I Loved This People

I Loved This People

BY DIETRICH BONHOEFFER

Testimonies of Responsibility
With an Introduction by Hans Rothfels

TRANSLATED BY KEITH R. CRIM

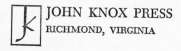

JOHN KNOX PRESS
RICHMOND, VIRGINIA

A translation of *Ich habe dieses Volk geliebt*, by
Dietrich Bonhoeffer, published by Chr. Kaiser Verlag,
München, Germany, 1964.

Second printing 1966

Library of Congress Catalog Card Number: 65-15715
© M. E. Bratcher 1965
Printed in the United States of America
3681(WB)9822

BY WAY OF INTRODUCTION

In the sketch "After Ten Years," which is the nucleus of these testimonies from the pen of Dietrich Bonhoeffer, presented here in brief selection, we hear at the very beginning the main motif, the word of the "responsible life." And shortly thereafter it is said that what we Germans still lack is the "decisive basic insight . . . of the necessity of free, responsible action, even in opposition to calling and commission." Only the "free risk of faith in responsible action" can withstand the great "masquerade of evil" which throws all ethical concepts into confusion.

The man who wrote these words toward the beginning of the year 1943 was, at the time Hitler seized power, lecturer in the University of Berlin and student pastor at the technical college. Twenty-seven years old, he immediately took the most uncompromising position in the church struggle which was then beginning. In the autumn of 1933 he assumed the foreign pastorate in London. That could easily have been an occasion for withdrawing to responsibility within the normal limits of "calling and commission." In reality both of these, and also the "free

risk of faith," placed Bonhoeffer in the forefront of
the Christian community which was brought together
in opposition to the approaching calamity, the appearance of the "beast out of the abyss." In particular, the time in London was the basis of the intimate
relationship of trust with the Bishop of Chichester.
In the middle of the war (1942) a significant attempt
was made through this relationship to establish a
bridge between the "other Germany" and the enemy
powers. That was political conspiracy undertaken in
love for the German people and in uncompromising
opposition to godless and criminal authority. It had
had its prelude in the realm of church affairs when
Bonhoeffer was called in 1935 to the leadership of the
school for preachers of the Confessing Church in
Finkenwalde. According to all traditional concepts
this was a very extraordinary and illegal organiza-
tion, which, for the sake of the educational task, was
already taking on the form of political conspiracy,
and which seemed scarcely to correspond to the
priestly calling.

Once again Bonhoeffer was given an opportunity to
escape the consequences of the path he was following
and of his nature, which was a unique union of mani-
fold and natural richness of spiritual and artistic gifts
with total moral commitment. In 1939 he was invited
to make a lecture tour in the United States. There he
was offered residence, a position, and a professorship.
This was the summer of the high political tension before the outbreak of the war. In a clear and calm

decision Bonhoeffer chose to return. In the sketches in his diary before and during the return voyage he wrote in this connection, "Above all I miss Germany and the brethren . . . I do not understand why I am here. . . . The brief prayer in which we thought of the German brethren almost overwhelmed me. . . . In case of war I do not want to be here. . . . Since I have been on board ship my inward indecisiveness about the future has ceased." And later from his prison cell he wrote to his friend Eberhard Bethge, "I regard the fact that I now sit here as my participation in the fate of Germany, on which I had already determined. . . ." This determination led him not only to prominent participation in the church struggle, especially as a connecting link in the international Christian front, but together with his brother and his two brothers-in-law, also into the inner circle of active political opposition, which had its backing in the defense section of the supreme command of the *Wehrmacht,* specifically around General Oster, who had decided on a radical break. In April 1943 the Gestapo took action, and two years later Dietrich Bonhoeffer's fate was fulfilled in the Flossenbürg concentration camp. During the time of his imprisonment he busied himself with theological and philosophical compositions, especially with the completion of his *Ethics.* The letters and poems which he wrote down in prison also belong to the most powerful testimonies *ex tenebris.* It is not without consideration of this fact that this present selection is primarily made up of documents from the time of his imprisonment. "After Ten Years" holds its special position not only as a contribution to Christian ethics, but also because here someone in the midst of the task of political resistance, not after imprisonment or in retrospective remembrance, is presenting to his co-workers in an accountable manner the inner basis for common action. There is surely no other testimony of this sort from the active days themselves which so impressively bears witness to the inward ties to Germany, and at the same time does not shrink from speaking of the "experience of betrayal," which almost no one was spared. Here we are really touching on the most deeply moving and obligating motives of resistance in the freedom of responsible deed.

Hans Rothfels
Tübingen, July 1961

CONTENTS

I   Letters to a Young Man   11

II   After Ten Years   17

III   Confession of Guilt   39

IV   Incomplete Draft from the Year 1942 of
a Proclamation from the Pulpit
After a Political Overthrow   45

V   From a Fragment of a Drama   49

VI   Night Voices   51

About This Collection   61

I *Letters to a Young Man*

17 November 1941

Dear C.,

It was really quite a surprise to get your package. I wish I could see you again and listen to what you have to say. You are now having your own experiences, and they are completely different from the ones I had when I was your age. I really believe that a great deal depends on what one experiences in his twenties, and above all on how he experiences it. For me those were the years around 1926. My studies were about over; it was possible to study and work in complete freedom; you could travel and see something of Europe. Europe was then gradually recovering once more from the poverty, the divisions, and the hatred which the World War had brought with it. Germany was beginning to earn again a place in the world through work, science, and spirit. Old prejudices of the peoples against one another were giving way to a hope that was rising among the peoples of the West for a better, more fruitful life together in a spirit of peace. The best forces of the peoples were striving to achieve the peace—which to be sure was

from the start greatly threatened. One sensed something like an occidental task, even mission, in the
world. One worked and thought he knew what he
was working for. Circles were formed that were serious and knew themselves to be intellectually responsible.

People discussed passionately in opposition to, and
then finally together with, one another. I could continue at length, and you will understand that in such
reminiscences my heart is not uninvolved. But I understand too that for you this world no longer exists.
You will say, "illusions, romanticism, dreams." You
see other things and think perhaps that what you see
and experience is now the real world, just as we
thought then. One is probably as correct and as false
as the other. Perhaps I can express it like this. The
demands of the present on you are so great that you
have little curiosity, and perhaps also little energy to
think of the future, to make plans. We were so taken
up with the future that in many respects we passed
a decisively false judgment on the present. Now I
believe that before too much longer both will be
equally necessary: men who will look at the present
soberly, and who yet do not give up the future—it too
is a part of reality! Irresponsibility in respect to the
future is nihilism, and irresponsibility in respect to
the present is fanaticism. We must overcome them
both, and in this task, which is also a highly personal
one, we can and must finally unite, however different the background of our experiences is. It is my

firm conviction, and also my experience from conversation with many persons, that today no one can look the present straight in the eye, and at the same time have strength for future tasks, who does not believe in the Creator—and the Redeemer. . . . It would be good to talk about this some time. Perhaps in doing so we would discover that we are speaking of the same matter with very different words, and have the same goal in mind. But then perhaps not. Now, enough of this. Good-bye, C. May God protect you wherever you are. All good wishes and hearty greetings from

Your Dietrich Bonhoeffer

18 June 1942

Dear C.,

E. told me a few days ago that today is your birthday. I wanted to send you greetings, and now this trip has finally given me the leisure to do so. As I ride in the beautiful sunshine through old cities and the summer countryside I am thinking of you, of your present life, and of your future. What should I really write to you? What kind of thoughts and wishes can I have for you? In years you are younger than I am by half a man's age, and by the rapid passage of time, by at least a generation. You are experiencing and

doing and thinking things which I have never experienced, done, or thought. You are in dangers that are
unknown to me. I am leading a life that resembles
yours in scarcely anything, and which must seem
strange to you. And yet, precisely this long journey
through our beautiful country, the glimpses of the
cathedrals of Naumburg, Bamberg, and Nürn-
berg, of the tilled fields, in part so infertile, and the
thought that all this has been the field of work and
the joy of many, many generations, give me the confidence that here there is yet some common ground,
a common task, a common hope, and therefore something that can bridge the chasm between the generations. When one thinks of this then one's own short
personal life seems relatively unimportant and one
begins to think in terms of greater spans of time and
greater tasks. You are at present a member of a society
that is surely taking part in one of the great transi-
tions of history. You yourself can do scarcely anything for the total course of affairs, and you probably
often feel quite superfluous and out of place, and
have all sorts of personal sorrows and struggles. What
more could I wish for you than that you should
learn not to take these little personal matters, wishes,
and concerns too seriously, but understand that you
are, in your own place and in the possibilities given
to you, a member in the long sequence of those generations which have labored and lived for a beautiful,
genuine—and devout—Germany, and do so still? It
is not at all true that you cannot do anything in this

connection, even though it is less your activity than your being that is decisive here. How tremendous the tasks will be when the battle can no longer be waged outwardly, but all our strength can be given to inward upbuilding. For this we will some day need not only performance and ability, but above all genuine men. And even if you only understand the present period of your life as God's intending to make out of you now the man whom he will use at a later time, and whom he will put to work with all the abilities and gifts given him, then much has already been gained! And now it all depends on whether we who at present feel that we are not being fully used, not fully put to work—and in this we share a common experience—whether we let ourselves be prepared through this time for the future. It may be quite good for us to be laid aside for a time and not taken seriously. Through this we could learn modesty and patience, and also faithfulness. And if in this time God wants to make of us devout men whom he can one day use, then we can be very thankful to him for this time. Now may God protect you in body and soul. Greetings in faithful remembrance from

Your Dietrich Bonhoeffer

II *After Ten Years*

Ten years are a long time in the life of any man. Because time is the most precious thing at our disposal, in that it cannot be brought back again, each time we look back the thought disquiets us that perhaps this was lost time. Time would be lost in which we had not lived as men, had experiences, learned, created, enjoyed, and suffered. Lost time is unfilled, empty time. The past years were certainly not that. We have lost immeasurably much, but the time was not lost. To be sure, knowledge and experience of which one subsequently becomes conscious are only abstractions of reality, of life itself as it was lived. But while being able to forget may be a blessing, memory, the repetition of lessons we have received, is yet a part of responsible life. In the following pages I would like to try to give an account of some of those things which in these times have pressed in upon us as common discoveries and knowledge, not personal experiences, not something arranged systematically, not discussions and theories, but results which were to some extent shared in the circle of like-minded persons in the realm of human affairs, brought together, but belonging to each other only on the basis of concrete experience; nothing new is here, but things known for long in the past, and yet given to us anew to experience and perceive. It is impossible to write about these things without there being a feeling of thankfulness for all the community of spirit and of life that was preserved and proved in these years, accompanying every word.

NO GROUND UNDER OUR FEET

Have there ever in history been men who had in their own time so little ground under their feet—for whom all present alternatives in the realm of the possible appeared at once as unbearable, so inimical to life, so senseless; who beyond all these present alternatives sought the source of their strength so completely in the past and in the future; and who yet, without being visionaries, could wait so confidently and quietly for the success of their cause as we? Or rather, have the responsible thinkers of a generation facing a great historical turning point ever felt differently from the way we do today—precisely because something new was coming into being that did not coincide with the alternatives of the present?

WHO STANDS FIRM?

The great masquerade of evil has thrown all ethical concepts into confusion. It is completely confusing for one who comes from our world of traditional ethical concepts that evil appears in the form of light, of good deeds, of historical necessity, of social righteousness; for the Christian, who lives with the Bible, this situation is precisely a confirmation of the wicked abyss of evil.

The failure of the "rational" persons, who think they are able by a little reasonableness to (with the best intentions and a naïve misunderstanding of reality) put back together the pillars that have come to pieces, is obvious. With their inadequate ability to see, they want to do justice to all sides and are then crushed by the forces which are rebounding on one another, and do not accomplish the slightest result. Disappointed by the irrationality of the world, they see themselves doomed to futility, and resignedly they step aside or fall an easy victim to those who are stronger.

More overwhelming is the shattering of all ethical "fanaticism." The fanatic thinks he can oppose the power of evil with the purity of a principle. But like the bull, he thrusts at the red cloth instead of the one who carries it, grows tired, and is defeated. He becomes entangled in nonessentials and falls into the trap of the one who is cleverer than he is.

Lonely, the man of "conscience" resists the superior force of the situation which demands a decision. But the extent of the conflicts in which he has to make a choice, guided and supported by nothing except his own conscience, tears him to pieces. The innumerable honorable and seductive disguises in which evil approaches him make his conscience fearful and uncertain, until he is finally satisfied with having a

salved conscience instead of a good one, until he
therefore deceives his own conscience in order not to
despair. For the man whose only support is his conscience can never grasp the fact that a bad conscience can be stronger and more healthy than a de-
ceived conscience.

The sure path of "duty" seems to lead out of the
confusing mass of possible decisions. Here what is
commanded is seized upon as the most certain. The
responsibility for the command is borne by the one
who issues it, not by the one who carries it out. But
in being limited to what accords with duty, one never
comes to the boldness of a deed that leads to personal
responsibility, that alone can strike at the center
of evil and overcome it. The man of duty will finally
be obliged to fulfill his duty even to the devil.

But whoever undertakes in his personal "freedom"
to stand as a man in the world, who values the necessary deed more highly than the purity of his own
conscience and reputation, who is ready to sacrifice
a futile principle for a fruitful compromise, or a futile wisdom of moderation to fruitful radicalism, let
him take care that his freedom does not cause him to
fall. He agrees to the bad in order to avoid the worse,
and by so doing he is no longer able to perceive that
precisely the worse that he seeks to avoid could be
the better. Here is the raw material of tragedy.

In the flight from public dispute some one or other
reaches the sanctuary of a private "virtue." But he
must close his eyes and his mouth to the injustice

around him. Only at the price of self-deceit can he keep himself pure from the spots that come from responsible action. In all he does, what he fails to do will not let him rest. He will either be destroyed by this dis-ease, or become the most hypocritical of all pharisees.

Who stands firm? Only the one for whom the final standard is not his reason, his principles, his conscience, his freedom, his virtue, but who is ready to sacrifice all these, when in faith and sole allegiance to God he is called to obedient and responsible action, the responsible person, whose life will be nothing but an answer to God's question and call. Where are these responsible persons?

CIVIL COURAGE?

What really lies behind the complaint about the lack of civil courage? In these years we have found much bravery and sacrifice, but almost nowhere civil courage, even among ourselves. It would be naïve psychology simply to trace this lack to personal cowardice. The background is an entirely different one. We Germans have had to learn the necessity and the power of obedience through long history. We saw the meaning and the greatness of our lives in the subordination of all personal wishes and thoughts to the task that had been given us. Our glances were directed upward, not in slavish fear, but in free confidence, seeing in the task a vocation and in the vocation a calling. It is a piece of justified mistrust of one's

own heart, and out of it arose the readiness to follow
the command from "above" rather than one's own
opinion. Who would wish to deny that in obedience,
in commitment, in vocation, the German has again
and again produced the utmost bravery and commitment of life? But the German preserved his freedom—and where in the world has freedom been
spoken of with more passion than in Germany, from
Luther to the idealistic philosophers?—by seeking to
free himself from self-will by service to the whole.
Vocation and freedom were for him two sides of the
same thing. But in this he saw the world wrongly; he
did not reckon with the fact that his readiness for
subordination, for commitment of life to a task, could
be misused for evil. If this happened, if the practice
of a profession itself became questionable, then all
basic moral concepts of the Germans were under-
mined. It necessarily became evident that the Germans still lacked a decisive basic insight: that of the
necessity of free, responsible action, even in opposition to calling and commission. In its place there appeared on the one hand an irresponsible lack of
scruple, and on the other a self-tormenting scrupulos-
ity, which never resulted in action. Civil courage,
however, can result only from the free responsibility
of the free man. The Germans are only now beginning to discover what free responsibility means. It is
based on God, who demands that the free venture of
faith is responsible action, and who promises for-

giveness and comfort to the one who in this action
becomes a sinner.

CONCERNING SUCCESS

It is certainly not true that success justifies even
evil deeds and questionable means, but in the same
measure it is not possible to regard success as being
ethically entirely neutral. It is most surely true that
historical success creates the basis on which alone
life can continue, and it is highly questionable
whether it is more responsible ethically to take the
field as a Don Quixote in opposition to the new times,
or, in admission of one's own defeat and finally in
free acceptance of it, to serve a new age. It is success
that makes history, and over the heads of the men
who create history the Ruler of history again and
again brings good out of evil. It is the premature conclusion of men who are slaves of a principle and think
unhistorically, and thus irresponsibly, simply to ig-
nore the ethical meaning of success, and it is good
that we are sometimes forced to discuss earnestly the
ethical problem of success. As long as the good suc-
ceeds we can allow ourselves the luxury of regarding
success as ethically irrelevant. But when evil means
once lead to success, then the problem arises. In the
face of such a situation we discover that neither a
theoretical and uncommitted criticism and desire to
be in the right, that is, the refusal to stand on the
ground of reality, nor opportunism, that is, self-sur-
render and capitulation in the face of success, does

justice to our task. We are not permitted, nor can we wish, to be offended critics or opportunists, but rather, from case to case and in every moment, as victors or as the defeated, to be men who share responsibility for the state of history. Whoever does not let himself be deprived of a share in the responsibility for the course of history by anything that may happen, because he knows this responsibility is given him by God, will find, beyond unfruitful criticism and a just as unfruitful opportunism, a fruitful relationship to the historical events. The talk of heroic ruin in the face of an unavoidable defeat is basically very unheroic, specifically because it does not dare to look into the future. The final responsible question is not whether I am able to save myself heroically from the affair, but how a coming generation shall continue to live. Only out of this historically responsible question can fruitful, even though temporarily very humiliating, solutions arise. In short, it is much easier to carry a matter through on principle than in concrete responsibility. The younger generation will always have the surer instinct in this, as to whether one should act on principle or in living responsibility, because this is the question of their own future.

CONCERNING STUPIDITY

Stupidity is a more dangerous foe of the good than evil is. It is possible to protest against evil, to expose oneself, and at times it can be prevented by force. Evil always carries in itself the germ of a substitute for it, in that it leaves behind at least a feeling of uneasiness in men. Against stupidity we are defenseless. Neither protests nor force can accomplish anything here; reasons are of no avail; facts that contradict one's own prejudices simply do not need to be believed—in such cases the stupid person even becomes critical—and if they are unavoidable, they can simply be shoved aside as insignificant, isolated cases. In this the stupid person, in contrast to an evil one, is completely satisfied with himself. Indeed he even becomes dangerous in that he is easily inclined to assume the offensive. Thus more care must be shown in dealing with a stupid person than with an evil one. We shall never again seek to convince a stupid person with reasons; it is senseless and dangerous. In order to know how to deal with stupidity we must seek to understand its nature. This much is certain, that it is not essentially an intellectual defect but a human one. There are intellectually quite able men who are stupid, and intellectually very dull men who are anything but stupid. In certain specific situations we make this discovery to our astonishment. In this connection one has less the impression that stupidity is an inborn defect than that under certain circumstances men are *made* stupid, or perhaps let themselves be made stupid. We observe, moreover, that men who live secluded and alone show this defect less often than men and groups of men who are inclined or fated to sociability. Thus stupidity seems to be less a psychological problem than a sociological

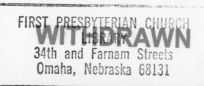

one. It is a particular form of the effect of historical circumstances on man, a psychological phenomenon that accompanies specific external relationships. On closer view it is seen that every strong outward development of power, whether of a political or of a religious nature, smites a large portion of mankind with stupidity. Yes, this has precisely the appearance of a sociological-psychological law. The power of one man needs the stupidity of another. In this it does not turn out that specific—and thus perhaps intellectual—human concerns suddenly are spoiled or go awry, but that under the overpowering impression of the development of power, man is robbed of his inner independence, and that he now—more or less unconsciously—renounces any attempt to find his own relation to the situation that has developed. The fact that a stupid person is often stubborn should not deceive anyone into thinking he is independent. In conversation with him it is felt that you are not dealing with the person himself, but with clichés, slogans, etc., that have gained dominance over him. He is under a spell, he is blinded, he is misused, mishandled in his own being. Thus having become a will-less instrument the stupid person becomes capable of all evil, and at the same time incapable of recognizing it as evil. Here lies the danger of diabolical abuse. In this way men can be destroyed forever.

But it is here that it also becomes quite clear that it is not instruction but only liberation that can overcome stupidity. In this connection we must first realize that a genuine inner liberation is possible in most cases only after external liberation has preceded it. Until then we must renounce all attempts to convince the stupid. In this state of affairs lies the reason why under such circumstances it is useless to seek to know what "the people" are really thinking, and why this question is so superfluous for the one who thinks and acts responsibly—only, however, under the given circumstances. The word of the Bible that the fear of God is the beginning of wisdom (Ps. 111:10) says that the inner liberation of man to responsible life before God is the only real conquest of stupidity.

Furthermore, these thoughts about stupidity have this element of comfort, that they by no means permit one to regard the majority of men as stupid under all circumstances. It will really depend on whether those in power can expect more from stupidity or from the inner independence and intelligence of men.

CONTEMPT OF MAN?

The danger that we will let ourselves be driven to treat man with contempt is very great. We know of course that we have no right to do this, and that if we do so we fall into the most unfruitful relationship to men. The following thoughts can keep us from this temptation, for in contempt of man we fall precisely into the main error of our opponents. Whoever regards a man with contempt will never be able to make anything out of him. Nothing for which we feel contempt in others is completely lacking in us. How

often we expect more of others than we are willing to
accomplish ourselves! Why have we thus far had
such extreme ideas of man's weakness and liability to
temptation? We must learn to regard men less in relation to what they do or leave undone than to what
they suffer. The only fruitful relationship to men—
especially to the weak—is love, that is, the will to be
in fellowship with them. God himself did not regard
man with contempt, but became man for the sake of
mankind.

IMMANENT RIGHTEOUSNESS

It is one of the most astonishing but at the same
time one of the most irrefutable experiences that evil
proves to be stupid and useless, and this often within
a surprisingly short period. This does not mean that
punishment follows on the heels of every evil deed,
but that suspending in principle the divine com-
mands in the presumed interest of earthly self-preservation works precisely in opposition to this self-preservation. This experience which has come to us may
be interpreted in various ways. At any rate, it seems
a certain conclusion from this that in the life of men
together there are laws which are stronger than
everything which believes it can be superior to them,
and that it is thus not only unjust but also unintelli-
gent to treat these laws with contempt. On this basis
we can understand why the Aristotelian-Thomistic
ethic raised intelligence to one of the cardinal virtues.
Intelligence and stupidity are not ethically imma-

terial, though a neo-Protestant ethic of sentiment has so taught. The intelligent person recognizes in the fullness of the concrete situation and of the possibilities contained in it the inviolable boundaries which are set for all activity by the permanent laws of human life in community, and in this knowledge the intelligent man does the good, and the good man acts intelligently.

Now there is certainly no historically significant activity that does not from time to time overstep the limits set by these laws. But the decisive difference is whether such violation of the fixed boundaries is regarded as their suspension in principle and is thereby declared to be a law of its own, or whether this violation is perhaps regarded as an unavoidable incurring of guilt, and as justifiable only in the immediate restoration and observance of the law and its boundaries. It is not necessarily hypocrisy if the establishment of right and not simple naked self-preservation is given as the goal of political activity. The world is actually so arranged that thoroughgoing observation of the ultimate laws and rules of life is also conducive to self-preservation, and that these laws permit only a very brief, one-time violation, necessary in a specific case, but they sooner or later, and with irresistible force, crush the one who makes a principle out of necessity and thus erects alongside them his own law. The immanent rightousness of history rewards and punishes only the deed; the eternal righteousness of God tests and judges the heart.

SOME BELIEFS
ABOUT GOD'S ACTIVITY IN HISTORY

I believe that God can and will bring good out of all things, even the most evil. For this he needs men who will let all things work for the best in respect to them. I believe that in every trial God will give us as much power to resist as we need. But in order that we will rely on him alone and not on ourselves, he does not give it ahead of time. Such faith must overcome all anxiety about the future. I believe that even our mistakes and errors are not in vain, and it is no harder for God to deal with them than with what we regard as our good deeds. I believe that God is no timeless fate, but that he waits for and answers upright prayer and responsible deeds.

TRUST

Hardly any one of us has been spared the experience of betrayal. The figure of Judas, which was formerly so inconceivable to us, is scarcely strange any longer. The air in which we live is so infected with mistrust that it is almost bringing us to ruin. But wherever we broke through the layer of mistrust, we found there the experience of a trust that we had previously not even dreamed of. We have learned to put our lives into the hands of those we trust. Against all the ambiguity in which our acts and lives have had to stand we have learned to trust unreservedly. We know now that we can really live and work only in such confidence, which always remains a risk, but a risk that is gladly assumed. We know that it is one of the most reprehensible acts to sow mistrust and to permit mistrust to be strengthened and advanced wherever possible. Trust will always remain for us one of the greatest, rarest, and happiest gifts of human life in community, and it can arise only against the dark background of a necessary mistrust. We have learned to trust the common man not at all, but to place ourselves unreservedly into the hands of the one worthy of our trust.

FEELING FOR QUALITY

If we do not have the courage to establish again a genuine feeling for distinctions in human relationships and to fight for them personally, then we shall perish in an anarchy of human values. Insolence, the essence of which is the disregard of all human relationships, is the characteristic of the masses, just as inner uncertainty, the haggling and fawning for the favor of insolent persons, and the effort to make oneself one with the masses are the way to self-degradation. If one no longer knows what he owes to himself and to others, if a feeling for human quality and the ability to keep one's distance disappear, then chaos is at our door. Wherever one permits insolence to be practiced near him for the sake of material convenience, there one has already given himself up, there he has let the floods of chaos break through the dam which he was guarding, and has made himself guilty

toward all. In other times the task of Christendom
may have been to witness to the equality of men; today it is Christendom that will have to intervene
passionately in the cause of the observance of human
distinctions. The result of this will be that one will
be thought to be acting in his own interest, and he
will readily be accused of an antisocial attitude.
These are the constant reproaches of the masses
against order. Anyone who is soft and uncertain at
this point does not understand what is involved, and
perhaps these reproaches are even right in his case.
We are in the midst of a process of degeneration in
all classes of society and at the same time at the birth
of a new attitude of nobility which binds together a
group of men out of all previous classes of society.
Nobility arises from and consists of sacrifice, courage,
and a clear knowledge of what one owes to himself
and to others, as well as through the self-evident de-
mand of respect which one encounters, in an equally
self-evident preservation of respect for those who are
higher and those who are lower. All along the line it is
a question of finding again the disrupted experiences
of quality, an order based on quality. Quality is the
most powerful foe of any type of degeneracy. In
society it includes the renunciation of the struggle for
position, breaking with the cult of stardom, a free
look upward and downward, especially where the
choice of the narrower circle of one's friends is con-
cerned, the joy in a hidden life as well as the courage
for public life. Culturally the experience of quality

involves the return from the newspaper and the radio
to books, from busyness to leisure and quiet, from being distraught to being collected, from sensationalism
to reflection, from the ideal of the virtuoso to art,
from snobbery to modesty, from extravagance to
moderation. Quantities quarrel with one another;
qualities supplement one another.

COMPASSION

We must reckon with the fact that most persons
become wise only through what they themselves experience. This explains *first* the astonishing inability
of most persons for preventive action of every type;
they believe, until it is finally too late, that they will
be able to escape the danger. *Second,* their insensi-
tivity to the suffering of others. Compassion arises in
proportion to the increase of anxiety in the face of
the threat of misfortune. Much can be said in defense
of this attitude. Ethically, there is no need to rush in
front of the wheels of fate; inner vocation and the
power to act are created out of a serious situation
that has already arisen. No one can be responsible
for all the injustice and suffering in the world, nor can
any one set himself up as judge of the world. Psy-
chologically, the lack of imagination, of sensitivity,
of inner alertness, is compensated for by a solid com-
posure, undisturbed strength for work, and a great
capacity for suffering. From a Christian point of
view, all these justifications should not so deceive us
that we fail to see that here is a decisive lack of depth

of feeling. Christ avoided suffering until his hour was come, but then he faced it in freedom, laid hold on it, and overcame it. Christ, the Scripture says, experienced all the suffering of all men in his body as his own suffering—an inconceivably profound concept! He took it on himself in freedom. We are certainly not Christ, and we are not called to redeem the world by our own deeds and our own suffering. We should not assume impossible burdens and then torment ourselves that we cannot carry them. We are not lords, but tools in the hand of the Lord of history, and we can really experience the suffering of other men only in quite limited measure. We are not Christ, but if we intend to be Christians this means that we must take part in the wideness of Christ's own feelings in responsible action which freely seizes the opportunity and faces danger, and in genuine compassion which does not arise from anxiety but from the liberating and redeeming love of Christ for all who suffer. Inactive waiting and silent looking on are not Christian attitudes. The Christian is called to action and to compassion, not by the experiences of his own person, but by the bodily experiences undergone by the brethren for whose sake Christ suffered.

SUFFERING

It is immensely easier to suffer in obedience to a human command than to suffer in the freedom of one's own responsible deed. It is immensely easier to suffer with others than to suffer alone. It is im-

mensely easier to suffer openly and honorably than
apart and in shame. It is immensely easier to suffer
through commitment of the physical life than in the
spirit. Christ suffered in freedom, alone, apart and in
shame, in body and spirit, and since then many
Christians have so suffered with him.

PRESENT AND FUTURE

Previously it seemed to us that being able to plan
one's own life, personally and professionally, was one
of the most inalienable rights of mankind. Now that
is all past. The force of circumstances has brought us
into a situation in which we must cease being "anx-
ious about tomorrow" (Matt. 6:34), and in this the
essential difference lies in whether this occurs in
the free attitude of faith, which the Sermon on the
Mount intends, or in an enforced servitude to the
present moment. For most persons the enforced renunciation of planning for the future means an irresponsible, frivolous, or resigned surrender to the moment; a few still dream longingly of a better future
and seek in this way to forget the present. Both attitudes are equally impossible for us. There remains for
us only the very narrow and often very hard-to-find
way of taking each day as if it were the last, and
still living so in faith and responsibility as if there
were yet a great future. "Houses and fields and vine-
yards shall again be bought in this land" (Jer. 32:15)
is what Jeremiah had to proclaim as the sign and
guarantee of a future new and great, in paradoxical

contradiction to his prophecies of doom, just before
the destruction of the holy city, and in the face of
the total absence of any future. To think and act in
reference to the coming generation, and yet be ready
without fear and sorrow to go any day—this is the
attitude that is in practice forced upon us. To main-
tain it bravely is not easy, but it is necessary.

OPTIMISM

It is smarter to be pessimistic. Disappointments
are forgotten, and you can stand blameless before
men. Thus optimism is proscribed among the intelligent. In its essence, optimism is not a view of the
present situation, but a strength for life, a strength
to hope where others are resigned, strength to hold
one's head up when everything seems to go wrong,
power to bear setbacks, strength that never leaves
the future to the opponent, but lays claim to it for
oneself. To be sure there is a stupid, cowardly optimism that should be proscribed. But no one should
feel contempt for optimism as the will toward the
future, even though he may be wrong a hundred
times. It is the health of life, which cannot be infected by disease. There are persons who think it
inane, and Christians who think it impious to hope
for a better earthly future and to prepare for it.
They believe in chaos, disorder, catastrophe, as the
meaning of present events, and in resignation or in
pious flight from the world they give up all responsibility for further life, for new construction, for the

coming generations. It may be that the world will
end tomorrow. If so, we will gladly lay down our
work for a better future, but not until then.

DANGER AND DEATH

In recent years the thought of death has become
more and more familiar to us. We are surprised how
calmly we take the news of the death of those who
are our own age. We can no longer hate death so
much; we have discovered something of good in his
features, and we are almost reconciled with him.
Basically we recognize that we already belong to
him, and that each new day is a miracle. It would
hardly be correct to say that we would like to die—
although no one is unacquainted with that tired-
ness, to which we must yet not give in under any
circumstances—we have too much curiosity for that,
or to speak more seriously, we would still like to be
able to see something of the significance of our past
life. Nor do we idealize death; life is too great and
precious to us for that. Above all we refuse to see the
meaning of life in danger; we are not desperate
enough for that, and we know too much of the good-
ness of life. Moreover we also know too well the anxiety for life and all the other destructive effects of a
continuous threat to life. We still love life, but I believe that death can no longer surprise us. Since the
experiences of the war we scarcely dare any longer
to admit our wish that he would not seize us acci-
dentally, suddenly, apart from what is essential, but

in the fullness of life and in the entirety of commitment. It will not be external circumstances, but we ourselves who make our death what it can be, death in voluntary assent.

ARE WE STILL USABLE?

We have been silent witnesses of evil deeds, we have been washed by many waters, we have learned the arts of deceit and ambiguous speech; experience has made us distrustful of men, and we have often failed to speak truly and freely to them; unbearable conflicts have made us pliable, or perhaps even cynical—are we still usable? Not geniuses, not cynics, not despisers of man, not cunning tacticians, but straightforward, simple, upright men will be needed. Will our inner power of resistance against what has been forced on us be strong enough and our standards for ourselves have remained pitiless enough, that we will find again the way to be straightforward and upright?

III *Confession of Guilt*

The church confesses that she has not carried out openly and clearly enough her proclamation of the one God, who in Jesus Christ has revealed himself for all time, and who does not permit any other gods beside him. She confesses her fearfulness, her deviations, her dangerous concessions. She has often denied her office as watchman and as comforter. By so doing she has often denied to the outcast and the despised the mercy which she owed them. She was silent when she should have cried out because the blood of the innocent cried to heaven. She has not found the right word in the right manner at the right time. She has not resisted to the death the apostasy from the faith, and she is to blame for the godlessness of the masses.

The church confesses that she has misused the name of Jesus Christ in that she was ashamed of him before the world and did not oppose strongly enough the misuse of his name for evil purposes. She looked on while deeds of violence and injustice were done under cover of the name of Christ. In addition she failed to oppose and thus furthered the open derision of the holiest name. She knows that God will not leave the one unpunished who has misused his name as she has done.

The church confesses that she is guilty for the loss of the holy days, for the desolation of her services of worship, and for the contempt of Sunday quiet. She has incurred guilt for restlessness and uneasiness, but also for the exploitation of the power of labor beyond the workday, because her preaching of Jesus Christ was weak and her services of worship flat.

The church confesses that she is guilty of the collapse of parental authority. The church has not opposed the contempt for age and the deification of youth out of fear of losing in this way the youth and thereby the future, as if her future were the youth! She did not dare to declare the divine worth of parents in opposition to a revolutionary youth, and made the very worldly attempt "to walk with the youth." Thus she is guilty of the destruction of innumerable families, of the betrayal of fathers by their children, of the self-deification of youth, and thereby of giving them up to apostasy from Christ.

The church confesses that she has seen the arbitrary employment of brutal force, the physical and spiritual suffering of innumerable innocent persons through oppression, hate, and murder, without raising her voice for them, without having found ways to hasten to their aid. She has become guilty of the life of the weakest and most defenseless brethren of Jesus Christ.

The church confesses she knew no guiding and

helping word concerning the dissolution of all order in the relation of the sexes to one another. She did not know how to oppose with anything valid and strong the derision of chastity and the proclamation of sexual license. She has not gone beyond a convenient righteous indignation. She has thus become guilty in regard to the purity and health of youth. She did not know how to proclaim strongly enough that our bodies belong to the Body of Jesus Christ.

The church confesses that she witnessed silently the robbing and exploiting of the poor and the enrichment and corruption of the strong.

The church confesses that she has incurred guilt with respect to the countless numbers whose lives have been destroyed through calumny, denunciation, and slander. She has not convicted the slanderer of his injustice, and thus has abandoned the slandered to his fate.

The church confesses that she has craved security, peace, quiet, possessions, honor, to which she has no claim, and thus that she has not bridled the cravings of men, but has furthered them.

The church confesses that she has violated all ten commandments; she confesses therein her apostasy from Christ. She has not testified to the truth of God in such a manner that all science might recognize its origin in this truth; she has not so proclaimed the righteousness of God that all real justice would have to see the source of its own being therein; she has not been able to make God's care credible in such a manner that all human management would undertake its task on the basis of it. By her own silence the church has become guilty for the loss of responsible action, of the courage of commitment and readiness to suffer for what is known to be right. She is guilty of falling away from the Lordship of Christ.

Is this too much to say? Will now a few who are entirely righteous arise and wish to prove that it is not the church but precisely those others who must bear the guilt? Will perhaps a few churchmen reject all this as coarse railing, and in the assumption of a call to be judges of the world seek to weigh and mete out here and there the burden of guilt? Was not the church hindered and hampered on every hand? Did not all the worldly power stand against it? Could the church endanger what is of ultimate value, her services of worship and her congregational life, by taking up the struggle with the anti-Christian powers? This is the way unbelief speaks, which sees in the confession of guilt not the winning again of the figure of Jesus Christ, who bore the sins of the world, but only a dangerous moral degradation. To be sure, the free confession of guilt is not something that can be done or left undone, but it is the breakthrough of the figure of Jesus Christ in the church, and the church must permit this to occur or cease to be the church of Christ.

Whoever stifles or destroys the church's confession of guilt, incurs hopeless guilt before Christ.

By her corporate confession of guilt the church

does not release men from the confession of their own guilt, but she calls them into the community of the confession of guilt. Only as those who are judged by Christ can fallen humanity stand before him. The church calls all to whom she comes to undergo this judgment.

IV *Incomplete Draft from the Year 1942 of a Proclamation from the Pulpit After a Political Overthrow*

God has not forgotten his church. In his unfathomable mercy he calls his faithless and tormented servants to repentance, to a renewal of life according to his holy will. And at the same time he places before us a task without compare. In the midst of a Christendom that has been smitten with guilt beyond measure the word of the forgiveness of all sins through Jesus Christ and the call to a new life in obedience to God's holy commandments must once more be proclaimed. Therefore we call all officers and all members of the congregation of Jesus Christ to heed this word, as it is given to us in all its fullness. We call to preaching. Proclaim and hear in all places the comfort of the love of God in Jesus Christ which forgives sin. Proclaim and hear in all places the wholesome commandments of God for a new life. Come together to worship as often as possible.

We call to personal confession. The oppressive guilt of long years has hardened our hearts and made them unfeeling. Christ gave to his church the power to forgive sins in his name. In personal confession we gain in an especial manner the certainty of deliverance from sin and of reconciliation with God.

You pastors tell your congregations of this way of grace and of this offer of God, which are now no longer widely known. You yourselves should seek brotherly confession and forgiveness and give to the members of your congregations opportunities to receive the grace of personal confession and forgiveness of sins.

We call to come to the sacrament of the Holy Supper. Receive in it bodily fellowship with Jesus Christ, the Reconciler and Lord. Receive also bodily eternal communion among yourselves as members of the Body of Christ, as brothers and sisters in the sight of our Brother and Lord Jesus Christ.

We call to community of brotherly love and brotherly discipline. Help one another aright that each may return to faith and obedience; show to the erring and fallen the way to repentance and to forgiveness, and walk before them in this way. Only in confession and repentance can we be helped.

We call you to prayer . . .

Open your churches for silent prayer. Let the bells ring for morning and evening prayer.

TO THE PASTORS AND OFFICERS

We call you to a new ordering of your lives. Long enough have we suffered from each one's wanting to go his own way and separating himself from his brother. That was not the spirit of Jesus Christ, but that of self-will, of convenience, and of obstinacy.

It has caused extensive damage to our proclamation.

Today no pastor can fulfill his office alone. He needs his brothers. We call you to a true daily observation of set times of prayer, set times for reading the Scripture and for studying the Scripture. We ask you to assume responsibility for giving help through brotherly discussion and through personal confession, and we impose it on each one as a holy duty to make himself available to his brothers for this service. We ask you, as preparation for preaching, to come together in prayer, and to help one another to find the right word. Gather together in confidence and brotherly respect for your superiors in the church; pray for them and help them in every way to carry out faithfully their difficult office. All who serve the congregation of Jesus Christ in whatever office should come together in new confidence for prayer, consultation, and conversation.

Be defenders of the pure and uncorrupted gospel and guard yourselves from heresy and schism.

TO THE CONGREGATION

Hear the word that is preached, use the confessional, receive the sacrament. Give free reign to the love of Jesus Christ, ward off hatred and vengeance, and bear witness through word and life to the Lordship of Jesus Christ. Let your homes be ruled by the Spirit of Christ. Gather around your pastors, pray for them, and help them wherever you can.

We call on the confessing congregations to continue to perform their service to the whole congregation as they have done thus far.

V *From a Fragment of a Drama*

In the second scene, a friend reads in Christopher's diary:

"I tell you to guard from misuse the great words which have been given to man. They do not belong in the mouth of the masses and in the headlines of the newspapers, but in the hearts of the few who guard and protect them with their lives. It is never a good sign, when what has previously been the silent and firm possession and the self-responsible attitude of all right-minded persons in the land is shouted aloud in the streets as the very latest wisdom. Those who guard true values with their lives, their work, and their homes turn in revulsion from the resounding words with which they try to make the masses out to be prophets. What right-minded person can still bring himself to utter today the defiled words 'freedom,' 'brotherhood,' yes, even the word 'Germany'? He attempts it in the stillness of the sanctuary which only the humble and believing may approach. Every one of us has shown an inclination to

49

these values; they are profitable to those who are
mouthing them today. Let us honor these great values for a time through silence. Let us learn to do
what is right for a time without words. Around the
silent sanctuary of the great values there will then be
formed in our time a new nobility. Not birth and not
success will establish it, but humility, faith, and
sacrifice. There is an undeceitful measuring rod for
the great and the small, for the valid and the useless,
for the genuine and the false, for the word that carries weight and for light chatter—that is death. He
who knows he is near death is decisive, but he is also
silent. Without words, yes, if it must be, misunderstood and lonely, he does what is necessary and
right, brings his sacrifice . . .

"What big words are these again? . . . Why do I
not simply say what I intend and know? Or if I will
not do that, why do I not remain completely silent?
How hard it is, speechless and misunderstood, to do
what is necessary and right . . ."

VI *Night Voices*

Stretched out on my cot
I stare at the gray wall.
Outside, a summer evening
That does not know me
Goes singing into the countryside.
Slowly and softly
The tides of the day ebb
On the eternal shore.
Sleep a little,
Strengthen body and soul, strengthen head and
  hand,
For peoples, houses, spirits and hearts
Are aflame.
Sleep a little,
Gather power, courage, wrath;
Don't spend yourself on tinsel and toys.
Till your day breaks
After bloodred night—
Stand fast!

Night and silence.
I listen.
Only the steps and cries of the guards,

51

The distant, hidden laughter of two lovers.
Do you hear nothing else, lazy sleeper?
I hear my own soul tremble and heave.
Nothing else?
I hear, I hear
The silent night thoughts
Of my fellow sufferers asleep or awake,
As if voices, cries,
As if shouts for planks to save them.
I hear the uneasy creak of the beds,
I hear chains.
I hear the happy lisp of half-grown boys,
Delighting in childhood dreams;
I hear them tug at their blankets
And hide from hideous nightmares.
I hear how sleepless men toss and turn,
Who long for freedom and deeds of wrath.
When at gray dawn sleep finds them
They murmur in dreams of their wives and children.
I hear the sighs and weak breath of the old,
Who in silence prepare for the last journey.
They have seen justice and injustice come and go;
Now they wish to see the imperishable, the eternal.

Night and silence.
Only the steps and cries of the guards.
Do you hear how in the silent house
It quakes, cracks, roars
When hundreds kindle the stirred-up flame of their
   hearts?

Their choir is silent,
But my ear is open wide:
"We the old, the young,
The sons of all tongues,
We the strong, the weak,
The sleepers, the wakeful,
We the poor, the rich,
Alike in misfortune,
The good, the bad,
Whatever we have been,
We men of many scars,
We the witnesses of those who died,
We the defiant, we the despondent,
The innocent, and the much accused,
Deeply tormented by long isolation,
Brother, we are searching, we are calling you!
Brother, do you hear me?"

Twelve cold, thin strokes of the tower clock
Awaken me.
No sound, no warmth in them
To hide and cover me.
Howling, evil dogs at midnight
Frighten me.
The wretched noise
Divides a poor yesterday
From a poor today.
What can it matter to me
Whether one day turns into another,
One that could have nothing new, nothing better

Than to end quickly like this one?
I want to see the turning of the times,
When luminous signs stand in the night sky,
And over the peoples new bells
Ring and ring.
I am waiting for that midnight
In whose frightfully streaming brilliance
The evil perish for fear
And the good overcome with joy.

The villain
Comes to light
In the judgment.
Deceit and betrayal,
Malicious deeds—
Atonement is near.
See, O man,
Holy strength
Is at work, setting right.
Rejoice and proclaim
Faithfulness and right
For a new race!
Heaven, reconcile
The sons of earth
To peace and beauty.
Earth, flourish;
Man, become free,
Be free!

Suddenly I sat up,

As if, from a sinking ship, I had sighted land,
As if there were something to grasp, to seize,
As if I saw golden fruit ripen.
But wherever I look, grasp, or seize,
There is only the impenetrable mass of darkness.
I sink into brooding;
I sink myself into the depths of the dark.
You night, full of outrage and evil,
Make yourself known to me!
Why and for how long will you try out patience?
A deep and long silence;
Then I hear the night bend down to me:
"I am not dark; only guilt is dark!"

Guilt! I hear a trembling and quaking,
A murmur, a lament that arises;
I hear men grow angry in spirit.
In the wild uproar of innumerable voices
A silent chorus
Assails God's ear:
Pursued and hunted by men,
Made defenseless and accused,
Bearers of unbearable burdens,
We are yet the accusers.

We accuse those who plunged us into sin,
Who made us share the guilt,
Who made us the witnesses of injustice,
In order to despise their accomplices.

Our eyes had to see folly,
In order to bind us in deep guilt;
Then they stopped our mouths,
And we were as dumb dogs.

We learned to lie easily,
To be at the disposal of open injustice;
If the defenseless was abused,
Then our eyes remained cold.

And that which burned in our hearts,
Remained silent and unnamed;
We quenched our fiery blood
And stamped out the inner flame.

The once holy bonds uniting men
Were mangled and flayed,
Friendship and faithfulness betrayed;
Tears and rue were reviled.

We sons of pious races,
Onetime defenders of right and truth,
Became despisers of God and man,
Amid hellish laughter.

Yet though now robbed of freedom and honor,
We raise our heads proudly before men.
And if we are brought into disrepute,
Before men we declare our innocence.
Steady and firm we stand man against man;

As the accused we accuse!

Only before Thee, source of all being,
Before Thee are we sinners.

Afraid of suffering and poor in deeds,
We have betrayed Thee before men.

We saw the lie raise its head,
And we did not honor the truth.

We saw brethren in direst need,
And feared only our own death.

We come before Thee as men,
As confessors of our sins.

Lord, after the ferment of these times,
Send us times of assurance.

After so much going astray,
Let us see the day break.

Let there be ways built for us by Thy word
As far as eye can see.

Until Thou wipe out our guilt,
Keep us in quiet patience.

We will silently prepare ourselves,

Till Thou dost call to new times.

Until Thou stillest storm and flood,
And Thy will does wonders.

Brother, till the night be past,
Pray for me!
The first light of morning creeps through my window
    pale and gray,
A light, warm summer wind blows over my brow.
Summer day, I will only say, beautiful summer
    day!
What may it bring to me?
Then I hear outside hasty, muffled steps;
Near me they stop suddenly.
I turn cold and hot,
For I know, oh, I know!
A soft voice reads cuttingly and cold.
Control yourself, brother; soon you will have fin-
    ished it, soon, soon.
I hear you stride bravely and with proud step.
You no longer see the present, you see the future.
I go with you, brother, to that place,
And I hear your last word:
"Brother, when the sun turns pale for me,
Then pray for me."

Stretched out on my cot
I stare at the gray wall.
Outside a summer morning

Which is not yet ours
Goes brightly into the countryside.
Brother, till after the long night
Our day breaks
We stand fast!

ABOUT THIS COLLECTION

The "Letters to a Young Man" were intentionally placed at the beginning. Even today the reader finds himself unawares in the place of the one spoken to, as one who belongs to this following generation with whom Bonhoeffer was here entering into conversation.

In these letters, the second of which was written on a journey to Munich to meet contacts of the resistance movement, he is already expressing thoughts which are then fully expressed in the sketch "After Ten Years." Bonhoeffer entrusted this to a small circle of like-minded friends at the end of 1942 as a Christmas gift.

The question of the last section, "Are We Still Usable?" could not be followed by anything more appropriate than the "Confession of Guilt," this so extraordinarily concrete liturgy, a witness to incomparable political responsibility, which must of necessity stand in the midst of these testimonies. The text was found in a manuscript of *Ethics* from the years 1940-1943.

The intimate connection between confession of

guilt and the "Draft of a Proclamation from the Pulpit" is unmistakable. This statement was one of the undertakings requested of H. von Dohnayi by Lt. General Beck at the end of 1942 as an emergency measure after a political overthrow, and on which Bonhoeffer worked for the section relating to the church.

The last two pieces, "From a Fragment of a Drama" and "Night Voices," which were written down in 1943 and in early summer 1944 in the cell in Tegel, belong to the literary remains of the final years.

The text is that of the extant writings of Dietrich Bonhoeffer edited by Eberhard Bethge, and the various pieces were taken from *Gesammelte–Schriften*, Vol. II and Vol. III, *Widerstand und Ergebung, Ethik,* and *Auf dem Wege zur Freiheit.*